A Kiss of Curiosity

A Kiss of Curiosity

Poems

Sylvia Dianne Beverly

Mill City Press

Mill City Press
555 Winderley Pl, Suite 225
Maitland, FL 32751
407.339.4217
www.millcitypress.net

Paperback ISBN-13: 978-1-66289-337-7
Ebook ISBN-13: 978-1-66289-339-1

Dedication

In loving memory of my devoted parents, the late Daniel Levi Beverly, Sr. and Dorothy Eleanor Beverly. I am so grateful for the love that you never stopped giving me and showing me by example true meaning of unconditional love. You both are poets and philosophers in your own right. I thank God for giving me you, you're the best!

Special Thanks

I wish to give a special thank you to Marquise Mix, aka 13 of Nazareth for being my first line editor.

Also, a special thanks to Charlemagne Fezza for her front cover design and being my second line editor.

More Special Thanks

Darrell E. Patterson
Grace Cavalieri
Doris Beeks Little
Allie Latimer, Esq.
Evelyn Hagwood
Hiram G. Larew, PhD
Kwame Alexander
Angela Wilson Turnbull
Diane Wilbon Parks
Andre BRENARDO Taylor
J. Joy Matthews Alford
KaNikki Jakarta Mix
Marquise Mix
Fr. Innocent Injoko
Dr. Michael Anthony Ingram
Takudzwa Chikepe
Dr. Thembie Tanya
Pat and Alfred Smith
Beverly Taylor
Dinahsta Kiane Thomas
Jamila Akil-Robichaux
Dayo A. Beverly
Misahra Briscoe
Cheryl Leonard
Anya Leonard

Drucilla Beverly Holland
Evangeline Key
Martha Ruff
The late Janice Sloan
Cassandra Rene' Calloway
Martin Vernon
Anne Harding Woodworth
Sally Toner
Liz Larew
Claude W. Correll
Curtis Crutchfield
Chip Kingsberry
Gerald Barnes
Lamont Carey
Sharon Y. Ingram
Benjamin Mertz
Jeffrey "Big Homey" Banks
Rev. Norman
Sally Jones
Kitty Templeton
Felicia Scott
Denise Marbury
Sophia Michelle Wright
Richard and Harriette Mosley
T. A. Niles
Brian Donnell James
David and Donna Nickens
Jan Brooks
John Ford
Alvin Carter
Charlemagne Feeza

JoAnna Howard
Jennifer King
Sydney March
Susan Schram
Joyce L. Moore
Rev. and Mrs. Keith Hopps
Brooke Kidd
Brenda Butting
Paul Lawrence Vann
Cynthia Brawner Jackson
Gregory and Alex Gaines
Jessica Thompkins and Family
Pauline Wilkerson Posey
Anthony D. Beverly
Linda P. Beverly
Karen M. Beverly
Donna A. Carter
Kimberly T. Beverly
Khadi A. Beverly-Diallo
Brandon T. Carter
Daniel R. Beverly and Family
Korin Dawud Agnew
Garikai A. Beverly and Family
Yazmina T. Beverly and Family
Habibah O. Beverly and Family
Ashia Beverly and Son
Daudi Beverly
Heamonse Washington and Family
Duane Kebo Johnson
Issa Johnson
Mitch Kesner

Thank you to all my family and friends, by the grace of God, who are too numerous to mention by name. Peace, prayer, love and blessings to you all.

Sylvia Dianne Beverly

Introduction

A Kiss of Curiosity

To God be the glory. All that I do is by the grace of God. It's no wonder I was at Davies Unitarian Universalist Congregation Church when I decided to publish *A Kiss of Curiosity*. I had already written the title poem to partner with the day's theme and decided it would make a great title for my next poetry book. *A Kiss of Curiosity* is a collection of poems that reveals more of who I am.

Since my youth, I was curious and not shy. I would ask what I wanted to know, especially to my mother.

Mommy encouraged me to ask whatever I wanted to know. This gave me confidence to do so. Mommy made sure we all had library cards and used them on a regular basis. I still love going to the library. Not only do I love being surrounded by books but going to library "don't cost you nothing."

Daddy brought us books. He and Mommy read to us and patiently listened to us read to them. Our first set of encyclopedias were "How and Why Books." I always loved short stories, nursery rhymes and poems. My favorite poem was "The Swing" by Robert Louis Stevenson. I memorized this poem before going to kindergarten and still recite it without hesitation to this day.

My mommy dear always brought our family joy. She always had unconditional love, kindness and goodness within her heart and soul. We were always friends. Mommy taught me many things and showed me the true meaning of friendship. Mommy was a poet in her own right, which aided me in following in her footsteps. She also taught me how to cook. My first lessons of cooking were making chocolate pudding and baking yummy oatmeal cookies. Mommy is my number one fan.

Lord, have mercy on me. Poetry is my passion. Reading and writing allows us to always have something to do. It's a blessing and a gift from God to share my writings. I believe there's a poem or story inside all of us. If you have thought of writing, go ahead and get started. Once you get started, words will flow like rushing waters of Dunns River Falls.

As we walk on the path of righteousness, to have and behold, keep expectations and desires on our souls. Hope is our anchor during these trying times.

I am happy to be a child of God. I am a queen, striving to keep faith, hope, and charity close to me. I am the proud matriarch of my family, praying daily to set a good example. My family is very loving and supportive of me, especially my sisters and my youngest niece, Khadijatou. My friends are caring and encouraging. I am a breast cancer survivor. I am accomplished and ready to fight for justice and equality. I am an advocate for the goodness of our youth and elders.

Foreword

Sylvia Beverly (Ladi Di) is a friend to poetry and a true poet to friends. She has a musicality that is only hers because it connects to every layer of her being. She has moments of tranquility and moments of persuasion, but there's no resistance in her line because she surrenders to her own thoughts and records them with generosity.

What is poetry but the human spirit? These words are a symbol of the poet's heart and mind. Sylvia Beverly tells the story of family, friends, feelings, and a true appreciation for life. I believe there's nothing created by nature that she could not see with some amount of understanding, beauty, or forgiveness. Beverly chooses words that are basic and concrete; she speaks the language of her time without artifice. The colors in her words come from a place of passion and joy and this is something she does not wish to restyle – she writes the way her mind talks to her and therefore we get a colloquial, natural, accessible poetry that can be reread with satisfaction.

This poet's motivation is not for praise or flattery; she writes because she wants to name the things she loves, and I cannot think of a better reason.

Beverly has her own particular range and dynamics in language that show her personality in every line.

I've never known this poet to be anything but kind, on and off the page. She personalizes her life in this book and lays it before you, saying, "I know who I am and I'm proud of this. Now I give you my poetry so *you'll* know who I am, as well."

Beverly (Ladi Di) is active in the poetry scene in her community and beyond. She gives of herself and, in our arts ecosystem, this is what we need to survive. We are all defined by our imagination and energy yet the artist has an obligation to contribute to the greater good, and poet Sylvia Beverly (Ladi Di) can be credited with this.

Grace Cavalieri
Founder/Producer
"The Poet and the Poem from the Library of Congress.

Table of Contents

Saving Best Wine for Last

Saving best wine for last
Feels good, forever hopeful.
Believe it: joy comes in morn
Keep looking up
Give, commit, surrender
A divine exchange
A relationship of love
Tighten up our thing
Jesus is the answer
A sweet transformation of self release,
Rejoice in the coming of the Lord
Receive love's energy, through
    Warmth of sunshine
Join in the goodness of the Earth
Feel bold and feel power of unity
Great is thy faithfulness
Make me an instrument of Thy self
A humble servant of the Lord
I belong to the Master
I love how He loves me
I want to know Him more
Read His word daily, day by day
From cover to cover, hover into His
    Word
Be patient; let anxiety fade into sunset

Enjoy beauty of faith, A great reveal
Still, there is much to know, much
    to see
Wait on the coming
    Wait on the return
Enjoy angelic smiles as we
    Stare into eyes of joy!
Saving best wine for last.

Safely Home

My heart weighs heavy thoughts of my love overseas in a war zone.
Bombs exploding at too close distances.
Day after day, we pray and think of ways to pass time away.
Unsafe conditions, unhealthy food.
Unmerciful timeframe to be a long way from home.
Family holding breaths, awaiting your return.
Wondering where, how, when obnoxious ideas entered our lives.
A gifted line of gab, a hole in one's head, a time to refocus.
Heading home cannot come too soon or soon enough.
It seems like forever, an eternity, a mighty, mighty long time.
It's hard; does not seem fair at all.
Doing your best, daily improvising all while there.
Trying to keep us from knowing real deal, how you really feel.
To this day, we will never truly know all you endured, on surface it's more than we can bare.
You are truly Sunshine of my life, whenever I am in need, you are forever there.
Such a sweetheart, you brought us lovely gifts when all we really wanted was our baby sister safely home.

(For Kimberly)

Hard Work Never Hurt Nobody

Daddy would often say laziness will
   kill ya
Get up my daughter, do something
   to fulfill ya
Hard work never hurt nobody
At the very least, you might get pension
   To help in later years to take care of ya
Find something you enjoy doing
Something fun and gratifying
Something you look forward to doing
Use God-given talents to easily
   woo ya
Enjoy yourself, have fun with what
   you do
Work it, work to high quality, work
   to best of your ability
No matter the taunting task, big or small
   do JOB well or not at all
We can always do more than what
   we think, think, believe, achieve.
Helping others we help ourselves.
Hard work never hurt nobody.
Great satisfaction knowing your
   work has surely helped somebody.

(For My Daddy)

Starving Children

Rise in defense of POVERTY!
Take action, join in or form
    organization to aid this
    heavy plight.
Do not look in other direction
Rise in defense with sincere
    affection, make a difference
    with a mighty might.
Nothing good comes easy.
Put in work, plant nutritious
    gardens, feed some others,
    do not give up hunger fight.
We can all do something, start
    Today.
We must turn this wrenching
 demon inside out
Unite in focus of people who
    have no food about.
Today, I learned there was a time
    mothers ate starch to give their
    stomachs a sense of being full.
Still this way of life, no food to
    eat, children going to bed,
    stomachs growling, painfully
    exists.

Rise in defense of hunger, feed
    starving children, save innocent babies.
Oh please, do not let children cry
    themselves to sleep another night.

Baby Love

Emotions run high, above tranquil skies,
rocks my world.
Life will never be same.
Just a week ago, I saw you for first time.
Lovable, adorable, great affection to my heart.
Currently holding you in my arms, exuding love's
sweetest six weeks of charm.
Horrid phone call saying you are gone.
Reason unknown to us, accept crib death.
Why, oh, why, we cry.
Holding in my arms one more time.
I know, I must let you go.
So hard to do.
Oh my innocent, sweet baby, a tiny baby casket.
I can still vision after all these years. So sad.
So hard to endure.
Prayer is our saving grace for sure.

**(For my beloved niece
Shani Beverly)**

A Letter to Self, Twenty Years Later

I want to thank God for allowing me to be able to acknowledge
   my former self.
Thank you, Sylvia, for taking on challenge of decluttering our home.
I know it was a super challenge, with professional help with strong
   desire, you accomplished this task.
You had to let go a lot and let God.
Organizing papers, books, journals, photos, cds, clothes, shoes,
   jewelry, knick-nacks, toiletries and household items.
It has made a superb difference in my life.
I can see clearer, breathe better, and feel freer.
Yes, to God be the glory at age ninety-two and beyond.

One Fond Farewell

One tear, One smile
One word before I go from you
The time has come that we must part.

One Fond Farewell.

We have learned a lot
We have made good friends
 now in the end
We hope to see each other again.

One Fond Farewell.

Our first level of education
Has been completed with much
dedication, now sincere appreciation.

One Fond Farewell.

We want to move along with
great success
We studied long and hard, ready
for any test
We will always do our very best.

One Fond Farewell.

A Kiss of Curiosity

Finally feeling grand, happy,
  oh so swell
Today, on graduation day, I bid
  to all One Fond Farewell.

(Delivered at my sixth grade graduation, 1961)

Thirteen Ways to Love Me

Pray with me and for me
Pleasantly surprise me
Share a delicious meal
Listen to me read poetry
Listen to me recite poetry
Hug me tenderly
Look deep into my eyes silently
Watch vibrant sun set with me
Watch full moon appear
Take selfies together
Grocery shop for me
Make me smile often
Make me laugh out loud
Give me flowers
Show me a pot of gold
at a rainbow's end

**(Dedicated to KaNikki Jakarta
"Write Like A Woman")**

Strong Roots

One mar, one scar,
A split in bark does not
    destroy my beauty
    beauty surrounds me, beauty inside
    me, deeply rooted, I will carry on,
    do all I can do to continue to aid
    my environment, beautify my
    community, enhance love of life.
    Emerald green nature wills me
    to breezy cool atmosphere.
    Spring has taken over
    deterioration.
Love warms path of
    righteousness.
I will carry on throughout
    summer.

My Dad * Honorable Man

I wanna honor my dad,
Montfort Point Marine
Doing what he can to gain dignity and
    respect for our race
With dignity and pride, bravery
    for sure, during World War II,
    he helped to integrate this
    noble branch of service.

Throughout years, with wondrous
    cheers, we thought strict
    discipline came from our great-
    grandfather
Now we know from gold medal
    and certificates he received, a
    a great portion of his style came
    from the United States Marines.

The few, the proud, "we are
    looking for a few good men"
Mightily fulfilled when Dad
    joined the Marines.

A force to be reckoned, neat
    And clean, shoes polished,
    hair combed, nice bright white
    shirt worn daily

Think well of self with strong
    dignity and pride, confidence
    will not hide, forever stating,
"I'm no better than anybody,
    nobody is any better than me."

Let it be told posthumously
    received a framed letter of
    recognition and appreciation
    from President Barack Obama.

Yes, Dad was a mighty good
    man, doing the best he can,
    working two jobs, all the
    overtime at hand.
Taking immaculate care with
    phenomenal love, ardent
    dedication for nine children
    and his darling wife.

Here's to you, my father, for
    greatness in you and
    all you taught us with your
    daily affirmations
"Hard work never hurt nobody,
    walking is not crowded
    laziness will kill you
    do your best or not at all."

Thank you, Daddy, for taking
    good care of me, thank you
    for always being there for me,
    thank you for your words of
    wisdom (even when I could
    not see)
Oh, Daddy Dear, rest in peace,
    know I will always be
    Daddy's Girl.

**(Dedicated in Memory of
The Late Daniel Levi Beverly, Sr.)**

When I Think of My Father

When I think of my father, I think of
    a warm, kind, loving, family man.
I think of devotion, dedication,
    honesty, high moral character,
    doing the best you can.
A hard working man, taking care
    nine children and his darling wife
Doing what was necessary to
    afford the finer things in life.
His only hobby was fishing, he
    loved it so
He didn't eat fish, never stated
    why
Oh, how Dad loved to see glow in
    our eyes
Each time he came home from
    fishing with a large cooler,
    sometimes two, filled
Dad's joy came, seeing how happy
    we were anticipating homemade fresh,
    fried fish, yum yum, nothing like it
He took pride in catching the biggest
    and only best, receiving citations
    for catch of the day.
When he was fishing, he was having his way.

All kinds he caught: rock, bass, perch, trout,
blue to name a few, without
a doubt my favorite spot.
Often, Dad would say "My oldest
daughter said small spots are
better than no spots"
Spots had to be a certain size to
be legal, seems like a mighty
long time since any freshly
caught spots were on my table.
When I think of my father, I think
of how he loved fishing and
didn't eat any kind of fish at all.

(Dedicated to Daddy, the late Daniel Levi Beverly, Sr.)

Kindness

Loving kindness and smiles fill
   the atmosphere
Pouring poetry all over us
A sweetness that God is happy about.
We are full of love, smiles, and
   happiness.
Oh, how we comfort each other's
   sorrows, we care for one another.
Kindness, we feel so good, we
   want the world to capture thrills
   of kindness and love.
Thrills come bursting through the air
   from sharing happy hearts of our
   Mothers' love our mothers' care.

(For Maria on Mother's Day)

Love and Comfort
You Bring Me

Basking, basking in sunshine of my love everlasting.
Every day you wake please know I love you.
I love you with overflowing joy in my heart.
You have a lovely, tantalizing charm.
Tenderly, pulls me automatically in your arms.
Thrills me with phenomenal sensations in pit of my core, forevermore.
Comforts my soul being, lifts my spirits to higher heights.
I've grown accustomed to being on my own when I'm not with you.
You are my darling, darling babe.
My Suga, My Honey, My Love.
Your smile triggers my smile.
Your laughter makes me happy and makes me feel oh so wonderful.
Does not matter where I am, what I do, as long as I am with you.
Walking in the park, laying on a sandy beach, watching movies, listening to music, standing on balcony watching gorgeous sunset or peering at the full moon watching the stars bring added luster to a tranquil sky, feeling like stars are shining just for us.
You bring me comfort, you bring me love.

This Love Thing

Then the lights went out.
Darkness fell across
    entire room
    I laid as still as I could
    on our silky, bear-skinned,
    fluffy, ivory rug.
I was not afraid, wondering
    should I be.
Safety is what we thrive to feel.
Alexa, play Smokey Robinson,
    anything by Smokey.
I can feel this love thing,
"Seeping in," great choice,
    "creeping in like butter on
    a biscuit," does raspberry
    jam come with biscuit?
I love feeling this love thing,
    in heat of dark, especially
    sexy, exotic rug is near and
    dear, warms springtime chilly,
    rainy night.

Sweet music, melody to my
    soul.

Lifts my spirit, ecstatic the
    lights will come back on in
    dawn of morn.

God's Power, Lean on Faith

Oh, ye of little faith, with
   God's power, our faith
   becomes stronger.
Faith, size of tiny mustard
   seed will move boulders.
Aid us as we climb to mountaintops,
As we climb through Falls of
   Dunn's River, feel extraordinary power of God,
   Our Father, our Creator, our Provider
   and our Maker.
Whatever it maybe, no matter how difficult, no
   matter how devastating, tragic, or impossible
   things may seem, give it all to Him.
Know He will do it,
Ask and know on Him you
   can depend.
Never worry, faith will carry
   you through as you look back,
   good and faithful servant
   looking back, counting your
   blessings, praising His name
   oh yes, you will see one set
   of footprints in the sand.
You will feel amazing grace, Alleluia!
You will witness God's power,
Lean on faith, replace fear with faith.

Ecstatic Twins

Praising God's name to
     an everlasting end Ecstatic, my dear
Happy, it's clear, March 13th is a day we share.
Uniquely, on this same day and same year.
     Covering global spectrum of southeast to
northeast.
You in Durham, North Carolina, country side.
Your Twin in Washington, DC, city wide.
Uniquely, we enjoy celebrations, during sunny morn
or twilit eve,
With family and friends, loads of gifts, surprises,
cards and flowers.
Smiling each time we call each other Twin.
Let warm spring breezes blow, Friends, twins,
don't you know,
We want friendship and poetry to perpetually show.
A friendship of admiration, A friendship of
appreciation.
Our heads to tranquil blue skies.
Strong in faith, we do believe.
     Strength in prayers we say daily.

Happy Birthday, twin!
Let sweet love flow!
Let golden, melodic chimes glow
     across the world, now and then.

(A Tribute for Patricia Russell-Hambersham)

Share Your Umbrella

A lifelong interest of mine
    supporting, sharing, caring
Feels exceptionally good to
    help someone else.
As we help someone, we help
    ourselves.
Let the center of our hearts reach
    out to others.
Wishing, hoping, praying all
    will reach out, do what we can.
"If I can help somebody, then my
    living shall not be in vain."
My Dear unity prevails.
Bringing power when needed to
    reign supreme, as we all hail.
Surely the world we cannot save
Bravely, we stand for something.
Help to bravely bring significance
    in clear.
Share your umbrella right here.
Here and now, do not be afraid
Strength will be given to aid
    as we reach out, without fear,
Share your umbrella. Share
    my dear, share!

(A Poem for Karen Maria)

Suddenly

Suddenly,
God called you home.
Tears fall from our eyes
    cause we miss you so.
We love you, Sweet Jane
We know you loved us, too.
You were a mother to us all,
Your family and friends.
Wise beyond your years,
    you consistently brought us
    together, whether it was going
    to church, gathering together
    to see the latest movie, super
    fun paint parties, out to dinner
    or brunch, at favorite restaurant,
    your home or ours.
Always and forever, good homecooked
    food, good drinks.
Not only a grand chef, a great
    bartender as well.
Oh, Sweet Jane, our angel with
    faith and love.
We know you will look after us
    in an even greater light from
    Heaven above.

For you, we are extremely grateful.
Because of you, we laugh a little
   harder, cry a little less, and smile
   a lot more.

(For our Beloved Jane Jackson)

Everlastingly Engraved in Our Hearts

Triumphantly, you stand as the rock
   of our family and many.
Always there for us with
Impeccable citizenship and
   character
Foundation of high honors
Building great promising
   platforms powerfully plentiful.
Rock of our family...
Solid as a rock!
Forever documenting history
   of families
Stronger, richer levels of life
   rises.
Showing how much we care
Teaching how sweet it is to share
Always in our hearts
A faithful servant
A Godly man, a real class act
A heart of gold, a charming
   sense of humor
Letting us know grief will pass
Letting us know to draw on faith
Heartbreak and anguish will
   not last.

Our rock, we miss you
You will be everlastingly
    engraved in our hearts.

(In Beloved Memory of Cedric Key)

No Matter the Season

An immaculate spring day
    on the Chesapeake
Basking in sunshine reflections
    from bay
Before we realize, right before
    our eyes
Summertime is here and bathing
    suits accompany somewhere near
Vacations are our sensational
    pleasure
Sitting on the dock of the bay each day
    Writing poems of melodic
    beats and measures
Moving right into autumn, leaves
    turn varied colors of burgundy,
    red, orange, and gold
Branches become bare, ancient
    leaves float in the atmosphere as
    they turn crackly brown and old.
Old man winter is upon us, each
    morning and night, we feel the chill in the air
Bring out crocheted, comfy, cozy
    covers
Lay logs on fire, light warm glowing fireplace.
Throughout all seasons, the sun rises
    at glorious dawn
Each magical hour, we watch
    amazing sunsets just before
    tranquil moonlight appears.

Shoot Your Best Shot

Since I was a child, I heard these
    words "shoot your best shot".
It still sounds good to me
    I'm always happy to be the best
    I can be, do the best I can do.
Whether a task is big or small,
    do it well or not at all.
Shoot your best shot.
All across oceans, rivers, yes,
    deep aqua blue seas, you gave
    your best shot.
In the end, your best shot did not
    bring you an awesome win.
A set back is a set up for you to
    get up, come back.
What a sweet difference the next
    day makes.
Keep trying, again and again
One day soon, out of the clear blue
    sky, your best shot will bring a
    phenomenal win.
Forever and always, my dear
    heart,
Shoot your best shot.

Amber Embraces Environmental Change

Amber, Amber, sweet, compassionate
  young girl.
Reminiscing on vacations passed
    while driving along the countryside
    of emerald pastures.
Spending time with grandparents
    on their family farm.
Oh, save our Mother Earth
Recycle daily, plant a rooftop
    garden filled with organic produce
Promises of a healthy lifestyle
    eating organically.
Amber cries out
Take actions, protect wildlife
Help arctic animals
Compassionate emotions stirred.
Amber cries out with polar bears
Please, stop arctic drilling
Please save Australian quokkas,
    extinct as they may be
Happiest little animals on Earth
Unique chance to see.
Embrace environmental change
Conserve energy.

Change Environment Change

Going green easily a state of mind in city of
    concrete jungle, going to be hard to find.
Planting trees, bushes, and shrubs.
One by one, under the warmth of the
    vibrant, golden sunshine.
Deciding to change environment
Going to take out time.
Fertilizing soils, plowing lands,
    planting seeds, doing best we
    can, row by row
Watering grounds, watching
    plants grow.
Cleaner air is found.
True to our hearts, a fresh new
    start.
Be part of a solution, help knock
    out pollution.
Cleanse our environment
Keep oxygen flowing
All across nations
    Just breathe!

Going Green

Answer blows sweetly in
   atmosphere
Stop, look, listen, slow down
   we will hear.

Time to do something to help
   clear our air
Time to do something to show
   yes, I care.

Time to decide how I can help
Time to step up and give one
   big yelp.

Yes, separate cans and bottles
   from other trash
Recycle daily and other rubbish
   will turn to ash.

Hope you are avid, young mister
Continue to help your mother and
   sister.

Praying each of us do our part
Going green will gladden our
   hearts.

Environmental change, reflective
 of a fresh new start.

Special Birthday Renga #1

Once upon a time
There stood a dear friend of mine
Grandest friendship ever.

Poetry, our first connection
Pumpkin pie and coffee, yes!

Love for family
Admiration for parents
Proud, true lessons learned.

Fragrant red rose, beauty chose
Nature embraced in our hearts.

Tall, kind gentleman
Imagination runs wild
Leadership with influential style.

Aquarius man, true blue
Happy birthday, dear Hiram!

New Lease on Life

Congratulations, America!
Excited a new day is dawning
To God be the glory
A fresh new day
A brand new lease on life
A mystery of sunshiny change
New beginnings for "America United"
United States of America.
We can see clearer.
We can wave our flag with hope, with dignity.
We can look to heavenly skies.
Miracles, wonders and faith supersede.
Beyond lonesome stars, reason to smile,
Head held high, Life and living worthwhile.
We have survived, plunged through chaos
     trials and tribulations.
          Finally, we hope we see a fair, fine future.
A future of great love, an amazing democracy.
Jubilant justice, everlasting equality.
Speak up, service with a smile.
Dreams come true.
Congratulations, with prayers for our brand
     new leadership.
Declare and believe an amazing democracy for
     entire world to see, from sea to shining sea.
Continue to hold strong to power of blessings
and promises.

(For Harris * Biden)

Unveiling Truth

Long awaited release
As we make an elegant transition
Alleviate our country from
    false loyalty and blood
    stained democracy, lifted
    up and ready to take a powerful
    stand.
Create major equality and
    justice across our land,
    hand in hand.
Unite in moments of constructive
    perseverance and energetic
    endurance
Greatly strengthened by youth
    of our families, our future leaders.
Practice patience as we approach
    decent corrective possibilities.
Humbly, we walk assured,
    grand gladness paves way.
Excited with dreams of statehood
    for our nation's capital.
Widely spread love each and
    everyday.
Praying for heartfelt unity,
Unveiling truth for the whole wide
    world to see.

(Inauguration Day 2021)

A Kiss of Curiosity

She was oh so inquisitive
Since a young girl, she wanted to know
She would ask without a doubt.
A Kiss of Curiosity!

A sense of satisfaction received
Always seeking an answer to her
    questions
Thankful her dear, loving mother saw fit to
    aid in her strong desire to know everything.
A Kiss of Curiosity!

To share truths to enlighten her heart
    feeling successful.
Loving to feel smart, intelligent, and strong.
Ready to lead, to teach, to help someone,
touches her soul.
A Kiss of Curiosity!

Determined to make a positive
    difference in our world
Reading, learning, obtaining
    knowledge to share.
Thrilling vacations, foreign lands
Soaking up culture and sunshine,
    witnessing first-hand.
A sense of purpose, a stretch of imagination.
She is committed to being a bridge
 over troubled waters.

Sylvia Dianne Beverly

Connecting with faith, hope, and love.
A Kiss of Curiosity like no other!

Today, she still needs a warm,
    sweet, strong, tantalizing Kiss!

Daffodils and Sunflowers in Her Golden Smile

Daffodils and sunflowers light up her smile
A smile, oh so sunshiny bright,
A golden glow of unconditional love, a pure
    delight
A love like hers doesn't come knocking everyday
A love truly guided her heart, her actions
A show of devotion, a show of dedication.
She loved her husband with all her might
    with all her heart and soul, her soulmate.
He made her laugh, his laughter made her
    able to make others laugh.
She loved laughter, a hearty laugh to behold.
She loved all things bright, beautiful, and bold.
Fixing gorgeous hair styles with ease.
Baking and decorating delicious homemade cakes.
Spending quality time with her sons, making sure
    they were always okay.
Thrilled by her hobby of collecting many elephants.
Perpetually, taking precious time for her family and
    friends of all ages.
A listening ear, a show of care, a free spirit.
In each springtime daffodil. Her smile appears.

Open our hearts, let love seep in each time we feel
gentle breeze of the wind, the warmth of the
golden sun, especially each Spring.

**(Dedicated In Memory of My Friend of 60 years,
Dorothy D. Waters)**

Poet Lady

She is here, there, she is everywhere.
All around, both feet on ground
She is a poet.
Confident, self-assured, dependable,
    oh so dedicated.
She moves with sinuous grace.
Curving, twisting, meandering
Taking her time as she sways and
    sashays at her own pace.
Quality is priority, even if she
    doesn't win the race.
She's a poet.
Pisces the fish, glide, slide, over
    under through rough waters
Build bridges connecting youth
 and elders.
Highly competitive, moving
    ambitiously into our future,
    creating new traditions.
Documenting our history
She's a poet.
Family, love, and togetherness
    mean so much.
Unity is very important, more than
    one way to keep in touch.

Sylvia Dianne Beverly

Glancing back to recognize and
 celebrate our past
Happy for courage and strength
 of our ancestors, oh how fond
 memories last.
She's a poet.
Perseverance, dedication, devotion, and love
Covered with hope and faith, giving God the
glory above
Praising God's holy name.
All He has for you is yours
All your successes are inside.
Got to stay focused to recognize.
She's a poet.
Yum yum, she's a chef and
 baker, too
Authenticity, pure and true
State your favorite dish,
 she will cook it for you.
Some like her sweet potato pie
 and TLC lemon pound cake
 best.
Others leave oatmeal raisin, chocolate chip,
 peanut butter, snickerdoodle, ginger, or
 sugar cookies to test.
Another fav is her mango salmon,
 how it melts in your mouth.
Try chicken and homemade
 dumplings, nothing but the truth.
She's a poet.
Work hard, play hard, reading good books

for knowledge and fun
Keeping a dream in her heart
Encouraging others to dream
Dream big, recognize, dreams come true.
Yes, she's a poet.

(Dedicated to Tom Krattenmaker, Esquire)

Soon Enough

Always and forever, I will perpetually
   be there for you.
Even when you do not want me to.
My sweet, beautiful, young flower,
Endlessly I treasure you.
Phenomenal, polished power keeps us close
   to one another.
Wrapped in blankets of luxurious cashmere.
You, my dear, are extremely important in my
Life, we are strongly connected.
Nevertheless, I will be there for you, even if you
become someone's wife.
Seriously, my sensational sweets, I need to keep you
   safely near.
For now, you must stay by my side.
Forever hold on to your dignity and pride.
As you grow, somehow, I will try my best to release
   you, my dear, soon enough, to find your
desirous niche.
Gracefully, you will dance into a cruel, cold world.

Beyond Massive

It's getting hot in here
H O T I am burning up
Stick your finger too close
    you are gonna get burned.
Since autumn is on its way, place
    logs on fire today.
Strike a match, add to logs, watch
    me crackle, snap, pop.
Seemingly mesmerized by me,
    I see stars in your eyes, you are comfy,
    cozy, warm, and snuggly.
On a sofa table sits a scented three
    wick candle, no need to turn on a
    lamp, I bring extra glow with
    Hawaiian high in atmosphere
I keep flickering!
Remembering grandmother's pot
    belly stove
Take bitter with sweet, I love to help
    make delicious baked treats.
Dad would say eggs love low heat
    keep me low, enjoy sunny-side
    up sandwich as you begin to eat.
Pondering need for fire drills, my
    presence said drop and roll to
    safest hills

Be passionate, approach stillness
  where it is beneficial.
Smoke comes from brush fires
Truly not my earnest desire
Wild fires burning, running rapidly
Destroying lands, homes, precious
  lives and memories.
Camp Soirée, campfire light, wholesomely bright.
I love hearing children and grown folks sing
All the glow I bring, specially making their
  marshmallows extra toasty and tasty.
Many times, you will see I am a show off of
  brilliance at night.
Please do not fan me, you will wave out my
golden light.

Voting Matters

You matter, I matter, we matter, voting matters,
    truly, truly, truly it matters if we vote.
Take note, it's serious, we must take minimum time to
    stand up in line and be counted.
Get up, stand-up, put-on mask with dignity
and class,
    take someone along to polls with us.
Assist with first timers, especially when they
are hesitant,
    remind them of our forefathers when they
didn't have
    right to vote.
We want change, we need a fresh start, exer-
cise the right
    to vote, express what is in your heart.
Let us be influenced by the righteous saying,
    "Voting Matters"
Pitter patter, pitter patter, peace be
    still, hear silent clatter as we stand,
    walk on up to booth, "Vote."
I still have hope, we all will vote, I am
    standing on the Word of God. Alleluia!

Cannot Wait

I hope and I pray when this
    pandemic is over, I will still
    be alive.
A long haul of solitude,
Forced isolation, seclusion like
    I have never known, never ever
    crossed my mind.
I feel like something inside has
    died.
As much as I try not to cry,
    try not to be sad, try not to be
    mad, feelings of loneliness
    strongly take my breath away.
I pray when this pandemic is
    over, I will dance the night away.
Jump with glee, be ever so
    happy to be free of wearing
    masks and won't need gloves to go
    outside.
Lord, have mercy, safe distances
    won't be of concern.
I can hug my family and friends
    again
When this pandemic is over!

(Dedicated to Michael Sean Headley)

Homeless and Hungry

Where do I go to be safe?
Where, oh, where do my children
    and I get a bite to eat during
    this pandemic?
Let it be told so someone can help
 our stomachs not to hurt
    So hungry, so cold at night!
My babies cannot stop crying
Fear and pain are reasons why
Change has to come for survival
    to remain.
Hard times drive us to be homeless
    and hungry.
Wide-eyed, innocent children stare
    in wonderment
All babies know are severe pains of hunger.
All babies want are a peanut butter and jelly sandwich.
How about an apple, how about a
    banana, a sip of milk, some juice?
Hear babies' feeble cry.
Listen how they whimper.
Can you please show us the way to
    shelter and food?
Food will take away pain.
Unite to help rid our hunger, help
    mothers stay sane.

Unity brings phenomenal change.
Thank you for the awesome help you
  give to get rid of gloom.
So my babies will stop crying
So my babies will have cover
  over head soon.

Faith Abides

Torment cries across indigo waters
Deliberate message flies above lofty mountains
Don't you hear our cries?
Sordid tears fill monumental fountains
Let movement continue past our pain
Let unity flow beyond feverish clay hills
Global massive demand of emotions
Bring closure and ignite policy change
A change so desperately needed
Serious thoughts of Rosa Parks
Horrid thoughts of Emmit Till,
    Sandra Bland, George Floyd, Terrance
    Johnson, Breanna Taylor, Jacob Blake
This is seriously sad!
Thoughts of my baby brother, Dawud Ahmed Akil,
    beaten to death by nation's capital police
Retching thoughts of our ancestors beaten, hung,
    strangled, suffocated, unable to breathe.
So much anguish, horror, and suffering
endured and still
    surfaces at will.
Continue to cry out, let our voices be heard
A call for equality and justice, a call for peace
A call for unity, a call for leaders to faithfully lead.
For all to replace fear with faith

Sylvia Dianne Beverly

Gather together in reverence
Faith abides, guided by our kind and loving Lord
and Savior.
Mercy, mercy me, have mercy on me.
Have mercy on our souls
Let us be strengthened toward righteous actions.
Yeah, a change gonna come.
The key is love.
Tell someone you love them today!

Southern Lovers

Love, oh, love perpetually tickles my exhilarated heart
Ecstatic to be reunited
Hour after hour we sit in handmade wooden rockers under
    giant magnolias down by the river's bank.
Silver strands shine and glisten our hair.
From dawn to dusk, delightful, darling days gone by,
    we reminisce.
So many stories connected and counted into a
    passionate, pleasing pantoum.
Remembering our favorite dessert, yesterday I made a
    Sweet love cake.
Three buttery homemade layers made from scratch.
Each layer spread with Milky Way nougat, stacked
    and covered in fluffy, creamy milk chocolate icing.
Generously sprinkled with our favorite nuts,
    fresh pecans halved, ooze like old fashioned hearty
Love and laughter, shared between lovers, with
each bite,
    each deliciously moist slice.

Smooth Spirits

Sitting proudly, Sylvia smiles, poised with
   passionate poetry.
Reminiscing on visions of yesteryear sonnets.
Floating ecstasies tunnels.
Special, sparkling snippets and shards of prominent
   pink sapphires.
Smart, pretty people sing sweet songs.
Pleasing Sounds serenade souls with sexy tones of
   shiny, brassy saxophone.
Smooth spirits entwine phenomenal beats, rhythmic
   pounds of snares.
Sensational couples sit perfectly still near
small spaces
   of private swimming pool patio.
Step slowly, sashaying peacefully along slip-
pery surfaces,
   slipping, sliding, push, pull simultane-
ously in step.
Serve self with puffy pillows, snuggle,
   praise each person's physical statute.
Sniff pleasurably, smell powerful scented
spices of sugary
   plum pudding snicker-doodles.

Where is the Light

There is no song to carry along
    for mental illness
Unless the melody is sad as
    can be.
In and out of gentleness
Forever struggling, trouble arises
Wanting to rid demons conquering minds.
Hollering out all day, all night
Rattling and chattering uncontrollably.
Sedated to stupor, over medicated.
Prescription not adjusted or taken on a
    consistent schedule.
Family and friends worn to
    disappearance.
Running from embarrassment.
Sad to leave love one behind
Still knowing feelings of
    abandonment is undesirable for all.
On outside looking in.
Wondering why thunderous
    cries are not acknowledged.
Quietly contemplating suicide
Feelings developed, absent
    from love.
Serious condition to be up under.
Pondering, wondering if sleep
    comes this night, will daylight
    ever unfold again?

(For Ed and other Kind Lost Souls)

Survival

Blazing...furious fiery red
Roaming...rapid flaming inferno
Vivid virtual violet
Purple passion reign on
    meek souls
Spirits rising to raspberry radiance
Fulfilling to rolling hearts
Crawling paths of dry deserts
Camel colored grounds to emerald overheads
No breath left, only mental prayer
Prayer sustains, tranquil darkness
    of twilight, leaves sparse hues of blue
Hoping for aqua mist to down pour of silver
sheen's shield
Mighty raindrops finally arrive
Awaken goldenrods of sunrise,
Fresh forest green fields of yellow sunflowers
    standing above all,
Swaying, resting to gather the aftermath of reckless
treacherous flames
Reflections of bright magenta splendor
Spirits smile
Knowing God comforts us
God guides us
God leads us forever more!

(For California Fire Victims)

I Cannot Take the Lashes

Thick raised red raw stripes
Puffed crisscross slanted
Scars for a lifetime
images won't leave my mind.
I cannot take the lashes.

Humiliated manipulated no control
Treated ridiculously for reasons
    untold
Tortured whipped hung strangled
    to death
Up under their horrid ridiculous
    mess. I cannot take the lashes.

Families separated never to see each other again.
Children left without their childish grin
For themselves to fend
Picking bales and bales of cotton on in
Working tired thin fingers to raw skin
    never to win
I cannot take the lashes.

Women left with no choice
Subjected to horrible force.
Doing what they can to
    accommodate

Never enough not to be sought after
    once it's late.
I cannot take the lashes.

Improper treatment, abused, confused, misused.
I cannot take the lashes.

Extreme hurt and pain
Limitless pursuit without gain
So much unnecessary suffering
So much disregard and disrespect
Dark dreary days degrading
No sunshine only rain
I cannot take the lashes.

I cannot take the lashes.
I cannot take the lashes gashes bashes
mashes crashes
clashes flashes of images before me
Ridiculous tactics of masters still dwell in our society
Living in a field of prejudice hatred and
mock democracy
I cannot take the lashes.

I hope and pray one day
God will take all prejudice and hatred
away
Remain aware
Remember freedom is not free
Stand for something strong and tall
Help your sister and brother if they fall

I am going to keep writing love
poems to help soothe us all.
I cannot take the lashes.

SPEAK UP

We must do what is right
Oh yes, let us unite
Purposely stand up for our rights
Through daily prayer hope might
Continue this infinite struggle
Use our poetic voices to fight!

By and by along side our children
We stand with grace and charm
Let us encounter for our youth, no harm
Infinite trouble across fertile lands
A server cause for alarm we must remain
    Strong, join hands, keep faith, link arms.

Peace be still, after you have done all
    You can just stand, it's God's will
Let His will be done, trouble falls by
    Wayside, precious jewels surface
    Sheer happiness eliminates trauma
    Burst forth with pride.

Humbly we speak, attempt to make a
    Difference, we can always do more
Beauty shines through, smile and speak
    Powerful, kind, wise words to score.
Take action, speak up!

Beyond Our Future

Standing on land where hateful hearts
    once stood
Makes you wanna holla for brute of no good
Early Early Rise at crack of dawn, slaving
    til dusk, throughout night still no rest.
God didn't make people to own people!
I know I am no better than anybody
Surely let this truth shine, nobody is
    any better than me.
It doesn't feel good in my imagination.
Actually horrid, brutal, rude encounters
    make me quite sad, sometimes even
    down right mad.
Going over and over in my mind, harsh
    encounters of my people back then,
Strengthens my endurance with a more
faithful loving capacity.
I can do more to encourage our children
    to assist our elders, to better myself
    showing up in our communities.
Being Bridge over Troubled Waters,
    connecting generations, uniting races.
Constant actions are needed, uniting with
    like minds, assisting where we can, being
    brave and creative don›t forget,
    document our history.

Live life at your peak, add years to your life
add life to your years.
Each day a mighty struggle our persistence
    remains keen, like Harriet, Sojourner and
    Fredrick our fight is for equality and justice
    unforeseen.
Today we mark our legacy, today we stand
    in future of yesterday.

"Sheros" Standing on Front Line

Free at last
Free at last
Thank God Almighty
We are free at last
As long as we know "freedom ain't free"
Freedom is a state of mind
I will not walk behind
Today, I am standing on the frontline
Stating facts and statistics
Speaking out with articulate diction
Speak up, let our voices be heard
We want respect, equality, and justice
No more prejudice and unmerciful deaths
    For our families, we want liberty
It has forever been and still is our quest
Perpetually stand out from rest
Let us all stand righteous, unite, do what
    Is best
Smile, always be kind, daily we pray
Prayer is our saving grace, lean on Him
Jesus will lead our way
Join forces with like minds
You can make a difference now
Don't waste your time.

Sylvia Dianne Beverly

I am standing on the frontline
Waiting for my next "Shero"
Step up, step in, step right on in
My dear friend, if not now, when?
I'm gonna slide to the side cause I'm
    A "Shero Maker,"
Standing, standing on the frontline
Until the Lord comes for me,
    I won't give up.

A PASSIONATE CRY

A passionate cry for FREEDOM
A surreal cry for JOBS with equal
    rights and equal pay
For I am still bound with iron chains
I pray for release, I pray as Dr. King
    prayed, for the power of Jesus reigns.

Influential, persuasive power as he
    stood on mountains' top
Proclaiming peace, courage, and
    justice, hoping injustice and
    inequality will one day stop.

Dr. King's eloquent voice
Gave many no choice
They joined political rally
Subjected self to jail, brutality,
    and horrible police force.

Feeling no ways tired
He would slide and glide
Over hills, over dales, over
    highways and byways
Making a way out of no way
Singing, praying, dreaming
Dreams here to stay.

His darling mother and devoted
    father were so proud of his lifestyle
Love of his adoring wife and children
    made Dr. King's living worthwhile.

Bringing many together and bridging
    the gap
Fearless drum major everlasting
    memorable speeches still flow
    like rap.

Peacemaker, strong leader, prophet,
    winner of Noble Peace Prize
Hope engraved in our hearts
    Help keep gleam in our eyes.

Holding on to precious memories
    of Dr. King
He gave his life for us
Oh, our great martyr, our friend, our
    reverent king!

Love Faith and You

Jesus is the reason for the season
Angels joyously sing as we shout
    "Joy to the World," praise His name
    "Oh Come All Ye Faithful"
Love, faith, and You.
All things bright and beautiful
Deck the halls with silver chimes
    and jingle bells
Lil baby, sweetly born to deliver
    and save us as we sing and tell
From highest mountain tops
Jesus Christ is born.
Love, faith, and You
Oh, Holy Night, a "Silent Night"
No room in the inn, a way made
    room for the Prince of Peace
Gifts of frankincense and myrrh
"Hark the Herald Angels Sing"
"Away in a Manger" bring joy
    and hope
With love, faith, and hope
Everyone is joyful, give love
On Christmas Day and every day!

Pretty Red Velvet Bows

Pretty wrapped gifts, red velvet handmade bows, wreaths,
    decorated with pine cones.

Gather dated ornaments, add polished toy soldiers,
    dancing ballerinas, precious doll babies and tin-
gling bells,
Standing in admiration, Nativity, prayers, and
grace dangling
    inside of me, with my soul it is well.

Wrapped in gleeful garland and tantalizing tinsel
Star topped tree brings special bells and whistles.

Hand written cards for special family, fans,
and friends
Old fashioned snail mail brings ecstatic smiles
and grins.

Cakes and cookies to bake,
Pretty as a picture after we decorate
Hot chocolate, eggnog, and rum punch to make
Singing carols at fireside
Exchanging gifts no longer needed to hide.

Children's eyes search elders' eyes
    To see all they can see
Fill our eyes with joy and love
    Let them receive happiness and glee.

Joy to the world, all the nice boys and girls
dancing, singing, somersaults, and fabulous
fun twirls.

Come all ye faithful, dreams of
a white Christmas come true
Let it snow, dashing and prancing
snowflakes fall from frosty skies blue.

Gee whiz, it's Christmas!

Suicidal

When one comes to this extreme
    is there really a choice
Committed by chance a final
    Recourse.
A shrill, a silence of death we
    wish not to hear.
Never understood how one could
    come to this space
Absent of feeling love, happiness, and
    Grace.
Too often to have witnessed youth
    to succumb
A recent college graduate or a
    young government worker
    living at home with a mother
Were there any signs of bother
Did they tell anyone of plans
    not to continue living any longer
If only test of faith was reeling
    stronger and stronger
What could be so horrid to
    cause grief and strife
What was the turning point to
    decide to take one's own life?

Melodic Pendulum of Love

Erase away pain
Erase away anxiety
Rid heart, body, mind, and soul of disillusion
Everlasting love of God, love of self
To thy own self be true, deliver thyself
Faith-filled love before we can love anyone else
Stay true to love
Keep righteous love vibes strong
Keep love going in a nation of chaos, confusion, and crime
Let love be more than an illusion
Amazing love, deep to core love
Like love birds perched on a swaying branch
Strike each other's chimes
A melodic pendulum floating through a tranquil mirage,
Filled with glee, sing a song, sing a hymn,
Exhale happiness only love brings
Our hearts sing a melody of love
Perpetually my dearest darling
Swing melodic pendulum of love.

(Celebrating Words on Wednesday with
  Miss Kiane)

Soaring

I wanna be an eagle
Big, attractive bird
Soaring high above
    thickest evergreens
Amongst cumulus clouds
    in tranquil blue skies
A mighty bold symbol for
    our nation.
Feeling free, far from earthly
    chaotic bother
Assured flight of next
    destination
Enjoying breezy mist of icy
    mountains in far off distance
Soaring safe, sound, sensational
    speed
Perpetually leading to heroic
    deeds
Helping to feed those in need
Bravely soaring high above
    extreme danger.

Early Voting (Haiku #325)

Great turnout at polls
Even though I must return
Hope grand change will come.

Faith (Haiku #208)

Have faith, no worries!
Show awareness, show you care
God is always there.

Compassion (Haiku #308)

Share feelings with friend
Sadness won't last very long
Sing a happy song.

Hopeful (Haiku #15)

Healthy nourishment
Whole heartedly enhances
Hopeful unity!

She Never Forgot My Name

Smiles when she first sees me
She is sweetly made that way
Always and forever best friends
Perpetually we felt a desire to be
    with each other
Daily, spiritually, lovingly, we prayed
    together
I prayed and still pray to have
    her spirit
To be ever so kind to everyone
A warm, humble, elegant and
    dignified lady, a humanitarian
She would often say
There's so much good in the worst
    of us
No perfect person in the world
As Mom aged, her mind would
    come and go
Through it all, an amazing
    blessing for me, makes me oh
    so happy
She never forgot my name.

(Dedicated to my Mommy
    Dorothy Eleanor Beverly
    1926-2013)

Phenomenal Beauty

Peering in an antique hallway
    mirror
I see life develops crystal
    clearer.
Eyes small and beady
Half massed, feeling a bit
    needy.
Nose spread across broad
    face
Fills my soul with heartfelt
    grace.
Smile crooked a bit to the left
Probably due to slight cleft
    lip.
Skin lined lifetime wrinkles
Would be more attractive if
    chin had dimples.
Phenomenal beauty shines
    best inside out
So, I decided to love myself
    no matter what else is in
    lonesome stars tonight.

Strong Sweet Love

Mountain high, valley low
River wide and deep
Nothing can keep Sylvia's
  love from you.

Oh, how she loved her
  mother
Oh, how she loved her
  sisters and brothers
She then loved her husband
  true
She loved her children, her
  grands and great-grands, special to her,
  each and everyone of you.

Dearly, she loved her family
  and friends.
She was lovely, sweet,
  strong, and proud.
Her grands called her "Fox"
  not Gram
It was her auburn and golden
  hair, they saw youthfulness
  and glam.

An awesome diva was she,
    forever let love be.
A love of care, a love to
    share,
A love that perpetually shows
    a smile there.
Embrace love in our hearts,
    let love unite us.

Be it God's will, we will see her in a
    higher place,
In a celestial space.
Our hearts may be broken,
    let us also have faith.
Hear her laughter, picture
    her smile, for now say, "Chow Baby!"

We love you, Aunt Sylvia,
    thank you for fun times
    "strong, sweet love"!
Rest in Peace.

(In Loving Memory of Sylvia Ann Wilkinson)

Faith

Oh Jesus, born the King of Angels
We believe in you, we strive to do what you want us to
We trust you, Heavenly Father
We are anchored in the goodness and blood of Christ
You are so strong
You give us strength
You give us courage
You forever give us hope
Let there be peace on Earth
Let there be joy to the world
We receive peace, joy, and happiness thinking of you
We pray to be patient day by day
To walk this earth in a godly way
To be with you on our minds
Keeps us healthy, strong, and kind
We are so happy faith leads each of our lives
We live with little or no strife
For you, Jesus, are the center of our lives
We come to adore you
We love you now and forever.

(Dedicated to Harmony Hall Poetry Club)

Darling Sweet Angel of the World

Darling sweet baby
Darling sweet girl
Darling sweet lady
Darling Sweet Angel of the World.

Quiet, peaceful, shy nature
When she wanted to be heard,
She could be quite bold.

Full of love, a kiss of life
A bond between daughter and mother
Devotion, never to be seen by any other.

Determined and true, witty and wise
Sincerity forever shined in her eyes
She loved all her sisters
All of her family, too.

Endurance and might
Never to give up the fight.
Meek as a lamb...meek as a dove
Oh, so appreciative for
expressions of love.

Patience and heart of gold
Grins and giggles to be hold
Rest in Peace...
"Darling Sweet Angel of the World."

(In Loving Memory of Debra Denise Little)

You Are Love and Loved

Oh Jabriel, our shining star
We are so excited for you to
   be here where we are.

Jabriel, sweetheart, our first
   baby boy
We await your birth with
   jubilant joy.

Our spirits run high
Our expectations soar
God blessed us ten-fold with
   grace and love forevermore.

Jabriel, make sure you dream big
Let your imagination run
   keenly wide
Forever be for real, never let
   truth hide.

Stand tall and strong, self-assured, Jabriel
Your head toward tranquil
   blue skies
At times, feeling and believing you can fly.

You can be what ever you
wanna be
We are here to watch you grow, protect you, teach
you, love you, and set you free.

Jabriel, have faith, believe in God.
Always keep hope alive
Know charity, which is love, is greatest gift of all.
You are love, Jabriel, we will always love you!

Broke Not Broken

Nowhere to lay, nowhere to rest, nowhere to
   lay her head.
No bed to sleep, standing on
    meridian fear deep, a few inches from busy
    street, a mighty, mighty long time since she
    had any food to eat.
Appreciating opened bottle of
    water helping to combat her
    serious thirst and intense heat.
An act of kindness, an act of love, a show of care,
   but for the grace of God, I go there.
Sign she carried read, "Broke, Not Broken."

Racism is Sin

Lean on God for answers
We stand in despair we stand
 in desperation
Severe trauma and great
 challenges can be satisfied
Be faithful, fervent in our actions
Singing and praying together
Praying daily with all our might
Unity prevails with actions
Take care of the sick
Love our neighbors
Look after our elders
Feed the hungry
Shelter the homeless
Clothe the naked
We need social action
Strengthen our faith, Alleluia!
Peace, faith, hope and charity
Love, love, oh, love!
Speak up, especially in
 uncomfortable situations
Lead us not into temptation
Become fullness of God's
 commandments
Build upon a spiritual foundation
Dismiss racism, bring forth justice and equality.
Please know, racism is a sin!

Let the Wind Blow

Where the wind blows
There are warm, gentle breezes
Like a balmy zephyr felt in heat of
Mid-day summer
Soothes my aching body
Comforts my lonely soul
Delights my loving heart.
Tenderly reminds me of
 vacationing in Aruba with
  my darling dear family.

Where the wind blows
  constant in Aruba, no need
  for sun hats and fedoras
They would only be left to steady
  winds flying high across
  ocean-breeze skies.

Where the wind blows
God's blessings grace me
  with divine health
I feel wealth of my sole being.
Happy to witness, "Footprints
  in the sand," looking over my
  shoulder.

Where the wind blows
With each baited breath I take
There is a strong refreshing
     intake
Allowing mindful support for
     my challenged lungs.

Death of a Child

Death of a child is so very
    devastatingly sad, sadder
    than sad!

Each time I have experienced
    this wretched tragedy, my
    heart is torn apart.

I was only ten years old when
    I first ever witnessed this demise,
    my young cousin died from
    leukemia, cancer of the blood,
    he was only five.

Unmercifully, I experienced the
    death of a child once again.
Decades later, my six-week-old
    plump, healthy, cutesy little niece
    was found breathless in her crib.

They called it crib death, I call it
    unbelievable circumstance
    innocent, precious jewel now
    makes up His Kingdom, little
    children who make up His crown.

When we least expect, gloom comes creeping
around in darkness and cold of night.

There's an unwanted shrilling chill in the atmosphere,
a feeling you wish wasn't there.

An accident on the freeway.
Unfortunately, no one was wearing a seat belt.
My darling dear fourteen-year-old niece was in
front seat immediately thrown through the
windshield.

Broken heartedly, still feeling pain of loss of child,
it's not mild once again devastation,
death of a child is extremely hard to bare.

Happy Nappy

Time keeps ticking into
    future, are we using time well
First time ever I heard your
    award winning poem
Over twenty years ago, recited
    in it's entirety by my then
    thirteen-year-old Godson
Amazing tributes for Mom's
    eightieth birthday, one after
    another.
From memory, my Godson recites
    "Lord, Why Did You make me Black,"
    takes roof off the church.
Ovational, still envisioned this
    second, a marvelous wonder!
Makes me oh so happy then and
    now as he takes his bow
I stand proud as a Happy Nappy Dread.
Delightful and true in all I do,
    pleased for this time to say
    "Thank You" wholeheartedly to you.

(Dedicated to RuNett Nia Ebo)

Khadi

K My youngest niece
Khadijatou, kind, sweet
spirit

H Heavenly happiness she
has always brought our
family

A Adventurous spirit like
jumping off cliff in
Jamaica

D Darling dear
devotion I feel for her
since birth

I IT Person for Auntie DiDi
intelligence is keen!

I Should've Listened to Mom

I thought I was grown
Excited to leave home
If only for the weekend
Excited to see for the first
Time Big Apple, NYC
Wow, skyscrapers, Lady Liberty
everything
Driving over Hudson River
Riding, gliding, inching through
bumper to bumper traffic
Vendors on every corner push
Carts, produce stands, one-man band
Newspapers and magazines
In hand
Clubs and discos plenty
Later we will hop many
First time seeing Lincoln Center
Madison Square Garden
Up close
Oh my, walking down streets of
Harlem, there is Apollo, now
approaching 125th Street
Central Park, Times Square, excitement
Rising in artsy atmosphere
Screams, cheers, hip hip hooray!
Restaurants, good food, music,
Clubs, pubs, and discos, don't you know?

Yeah, I came home, real, real grown
Realizing why Mom didn't want me to go away that day
Realizing I should have listened to Mom.

**(R.I.P. Mommy, Love you
Always missing you)**

Mother Nature's Creations

Mother Nature, Mother Nature
Dear, darling Mother Nature.
You bring sweet, serene creations.
Sensational, surprising sunrise
  beckons us at early morning dawn.
Golden goodness of amazing sunset
Wondrously welcomes full tranquil,
  tantalizing moon.
Dreams for an eternity of man's
  best friend.
I love when my friends share love,
  caring for their pets.
Enjoying playful energies when
  companions run along fresh
  waters together, again and again.

He Waited for Her

Daydreaming, as far back as
    she could remember
One of her favorite things to do.
Staring out the window, viewing
    The tallest pine trees' snow
    covered tops
Watching squirrels hop from one
    branch to another.
Far off in a distance, a little boy
    hops on his sleigh, zooms down
    the hill.
As she peers over the sill,
She sees a little girl, dressed in a
    snow suit, matching hat and gloves
    shiny red boots, reluctantly ease
    to her sleigh, down the embankment
    she flies, screaming to top of her
    voice, eyes big and opened wide.
Happy, excited, thrilled the boy
    was at the bottom of the hill
Yes, he waited for her.

Three Mirrors of Love

In my bathroom mirror, I am living in Revelations,
  for God is light of the world.
I pray without ceasing, there is an expiration on
  horrible pandemic.
I pray to be renewed by pandemic's end.

In second mirror, in my bedroom, strength
and courage
  is what I feel, truly, brilliance is what I see.
Faith abides, takes over me.
I lay down all my burdens. I am an overcomer.
I feel comfort as I am lifted to higher platforms, beyond
  my wildest dreams.

Standing front of biggest mirror I bought Mommy over
  half century ago, she in turned gifted me, I
am smiling.
I keep sweetness keen, love letter in your mailbox.
I keep kindness coming, I bake cookies,
pies, puddings,
  rum cakes.
I keep love strong, loving gestures unconditional.
I sing a tender love song
I keep praising our Savior all day long.

World Beyond Love

Walking towards rhythms
   of world beyond
Peering Death Valley days
Are we still on earth?
Or are we just visiting dunes
   in sand?
I see syncopated pans
Two-man band doing all they can
Soothe by rippling waters
   bordered by blankets of
     emerald grass.
Freedom long gone seemingly
   thing of past.
Deep into ancient ruins,
Water trickles down mountain tops
   far in horizon where wind blows
     fiercely granular of sand while cumulus clouds
     hover peacefully above.
When is true love coming into existence?
Where have passionate people gone?
Seems no one cares anymore.
Sun begins to set, together we take rest.
We walk off into sunset
   hopeful of everlasting love.

Doting Boons

Dazzling Darling Doll Babies
Divine Dearest Blessings
Devoted Beyond Dedication
Before Delicious Buttered
Bread Buns Biscuits Butter
Brickle Browned Brisket Beef
Downright Delectable
Desirous Bountiful
Beautifully Divine Butterflies
Beckon Big Bold Bricks
Dig Deep Down Discovering
Darling Diva Doll Babies'
Divine Dearest Blessings.

Message to Mommy

Melodies pure and true
Sweet Mommy, memories I share of you.
Phenomenal spark of inspiration
Superb sweetness of pure dedication
Root of my soul's ultimate being
Significant cry for peace throughout world.
Mommy Sweetheart, no wonder you are my
favorite girl.
Oh Mommy, Mommy, Mommy, loving you is
food for my soul.
Folks still remember you as a lady of elegance
and grace
Oh, how I love your face.
An optimistic soul, such a lovely, beautiful face,
Suddenly, I remember how you would smile
 when you first saw me.
Oh, Sweet Mommy, you are made that way
Every step you would take, made
 a positive impact in the lives of many.
Showing examples of faith provides us plenty
Oh, I love how you taught us to keep our minds stayed
on Jesus.
Gives us an optimistic way of trust and reason.
I just wanna say Happy Heavenly Mother's
Day, Mommy

Thank you, my dear angel, for all your prayers. By your amazing example, I just want to praise Him, glorify Him, lift Him up!

(In Loving Memory of my Mommy, Dorothy E. Beverly)

Summer's End

Where I lead my friend, you seem to love to follow.
One good deed prompts another good deed.
I love walking in steady stride alongside you.
Casually, we stroll through the path of seclusion.
Enjoying tweets and flutters of blue birds and
butterflies.
Not a soul in sight.
Bringing a serene atmosphere.
Bringing a feeling of comfort to my soul.
Nature is calling, settling with my wholesome spirit.
Looking forward to change of seasons from summer's
green leaves to cascade of autumn's
vibrant wonder.

Mama Oh Mama

Mama! Is Master gonna sell you
    from us today?
Mama! I surely pray not, cause
    I don't know what me and Nettie
    Clisstie and Jimmi would do,
    would do Mama, without
    comfort of your touch and
    sweetness of your voice.
Oh Mama, we would be sad,
  sadder than sad, so sad, Mama
if we didn't have you.

Mama, will we ever be able to
    live our own life together, just
    you, me, and my sisters and
    brother?
How come, Mama? How come
    we can't run about and sing
    and play and be free?
Oh Mama, Mama, Mama, what
    would make a person feel they
    are better than someone else?
Make them feel they could treat
    them any old way?
Huh Mama, talk rude to them,
    violate their personal space,
    disregard and disrespect
    we humans, we humans, too.

Sylvia Dianne Beverly

What on earth did we do to deserve
  such a ridiculous way of life?
Oh Mama, will things ever change?

Hear Our Ancestors Speak

Hear our ancestors speak.
Be a part of history
Speak earnestly of truth
Help create a righteous legacy
 for our dear families.
Hold close to us virtues of faith, hope, charity.
Humming, singing, looking to northern skies.
Continuously, everlastingly, we got by.
Oh, hear our ancestors speak.
Praying, gaining strength, courage, and bravery.
Do things out of ordinary.
Give voice to our thoughts.
Thoughts need to be heard
Thoughts must be said.
Guide, lead, inspire our way.
Make way out of no way.
Think it, believe it, achieve it!
Nothing is impossible.
We can accomplish beyond
  our wildest dream.
Our dreams come true.
We can always do more.
Take noble actions, listen to
  voices of our ancestors
Our ancestors' voices strengthen
  our walk.
Hear our ancestors speak.

Sylvia Dianne Beverly

Swimming A Mile for Me

Honoring me feels like a standing ovation
Swimming a mile for me, a phenomenal
    Dedication
I am "Chosen One," they say I am cancer
    free.
Feels overwhelming, I try my best, not to cry
My eyes fill with glassy tears
Tears lay on rim of my eyes, run down
each cheek.
Tears seem happy, seeking celebration
    of my survival of breast cancer.

Honoring me feels like a standing ovation.
God continues to spread His awesome light,
His everlasting love. God is carrying me through.
Over my shoulder, I see one set of
"Footprints in Sand."
Floating in cool of autumn breeze
I fall to my knees, give thanks for my
    Friend, honoring me.
Asking God to keep her safe,
Asking God to let her feel good
With each stroke she takes,
Thanking God for her bravery.

Honoring me feels like a standing
    Ovation.

103

Swimming a mile for me.
I write this poem celebrating her
    Victory- celebrating my one year
    Anniversary of self detection.
She is a breast cancer survivor, too.
An awesome support teamer
    Throughout my breast cancer journey
Sharing from her heart with
    Kindness, knowledge, and love.

Honoring me feels like a standing
    ovation.
Let confetti flow across bright, sunny
    skies, west to east enlightening nations.

(Dedicated to Liz Larew)

Elegant Loveliness

Beauty of her radiant smile
Pleasantly self-assured
Perpetually looking to aid her
    fellow beings.
Passionate talent scout, keen
    bold, and serene.
Brash words placed tenderly
    joined at hip with extra special
    kick and dip.
Rings bells, whistles, and chimes
Dancing on fire, keeps us alive.
Grace our tender spirits with
    heavenly, healthy deeds.
Stepping gaily to open mic
    thoughts of dainty blouse with
    loads of tiny pearl buttons
Wondering, did she ever obtain one?
Sharing a unique collection of tea pots
    quite an impressive jewel to see.
Lovely, proper elegance forever appears
at Forestine's door.

Happy Birthday forevermore!

(Tribute for Forestine Bynum)

Crushed Dreams

Senseless encounters place our nation with grief and sheer disbelief.

Innocent youth snatched away from universe.
Dreams crushed under gun smoke.

Pours from tunnels and chambers of misused ammunition.

Heroic teachers, humanitarians from start, loving their students.
Throw their bodies over students
protecting them from wild chamber pellets.

My heart bleeds at thoughts of parents, siblings, and mates dealing with tragic madness tugging at our hearts forever.

A grandeur of grief, a lifetime of disbelief, wondering will we ever have relief, wondering why this happened this way.

Forever and a day, I pray someone will pass laws where guns are not easy to obtain. And...punishment will be capital!

(For the nineteen young students, two teachers, their families, and friends in Texas).

Righteous Love Does Not Come Easy

Essence of life fills my heart with love,
   a special kind of love.
Hearts on fire, mutual desire kind
   of love.
Oh, how love connects us to each
   other's souls.
Spirits unite, loving unconditionally
   keeps us miraculously whole.
Sweetest words we love to hear in
   our ears.
Ardently, dear to our hearts,
   sharing, caring never to part.
At first start, love is winning,
True as blue moon in starlit skies
Twinkling bright as my eyes in darkness
Shining like diamonds pleasantly
   dancing across room.
Keeping "social distance"
Oh, my sweet darling love, show
   no gloom.
Righteous Love Does Not Come Easy,
   especially during these challenging
   times of COVID.

Gracious is Your Love

Gracious is your love with all.
Tenderly kind, answering God's call.
A gent with humble spirit
Faith-filled diversity always in it.
Perpetually considerate of me with
      all my imperfections.
So happy God blessed me with a
      wonderfully, truly unique dedication.
Opening doors and avenues through years
      for great minority to shine, leaving no
talent behind.
      smiling through tears.
Gracious is your love with all.
Partner, friend, presenting sharing
      metaphorical visions with serene
      natural themes forever caring.
A friendship strongly embraced.
Only by God's golden grace.
Weathering storms, opportunities form.
Enhancing plenty, enchanting many.
Gracious is your love with all.
Things seen in you, my friend, is the way
Our world should blend.
Filled with justice, equality, peace and love.
Fun in sun, gorgeous magnolias
      swaying with poetry above.
Gracious is your love with all.

(A Tribute for Hiram Larew's Birthday)

Yummy, Yummy Pumpkin Pie

Yummy, Yummy Pumpkin is my fave
Whipped with brown sugar, cloves, and spice
Pumpkin, honey, everything nice.
Moist, delicious cupcakes, plump
tasty cookies, delectable pies
Even pumpkin ice cream and morning fresh coffee
with sweet pumpkin flavored cream, yummy in my
Eyes.
In my daydreams, I take pumpkin over squash,
Sweet potato, and bean pie.
Once you have pumpkin pie, you won't want
sweet potato pie no more.
Yummy, Yummy Pumpkin Pie!

The Collective

A Kool A Lay (Good Evening).
We are the Collective
We each have our own perspective.
Love Poet I am known
I have long since grown
Leaving no unturned stones.
Love Poet I am called
For love is not just a dainty thing
Love is heartbeat of our souls
Love is power, love lifts our spirits
Hour by hour.
Love makes us reign queens and kings.
Genuine heritage to unfold
Another bona fide future to mold
Glorious, factual reasons untold
God our Father we truly behold.
Listen to what God has for us to do
Promising to follow to thy own self
   be true.
Each morning we wake to skies of blue
Each day we come closer to "the color of new".
Oh Lord, we must save the children
Save our precious children.
For in the future, the children will try
their best to save the world.

Tread fertile grounds
Until liberty is found
We rock, we roll, we keep on
    pushing.
We are bound one day to be free.
We recognize, in our plea with glee
Freedom still is not free.
Rescue me
Rescue me
Oh, rescue me, con amore!

(Dedicated to Grace Cavalieri)

Date Rape

She never told a living soul
Not her darling mother
Not her devoted sister
Not her dear best friend.

Over fifty years later, she
    ponders thoughts of
        letting it be known to another.

Year after year, she thought,
    with devastating memories
    horrific invasion of her privacy.
Wondering why she never told
    a living soul
Why did she choose to keep
    This To Herself, For Too Long
    Carry Burden Alone?

Thrill of Your Charm

Sunshine fills lonesome skies
Happy to plan quality time together.
Soon, we will have a healthy, delicious
meal this end of summer.
I have waited forever for glorious loving
reunion with you, my darling.
Once we are together, we will be oh so
ecstatic and my heart will be filled with
warmth of your charm.
Sensational thrill of your charm.

Daddy Dear

I am no better than anybody.
Nobody is any better than me.
Daddy always told me, stand up
   for my rights.
Be good in character, keep morals high.
Dress for success, be neat and clean
   in stride of a queen with a Midas sheen.
Never, ever give up.
Be brave and courageous, striving for
   Excellence, forever learning something new.
Knowledge gained, you will have a clue.
Lift your spirit to help someone else.
Smile into sunshine towards heavenly skies,
   basking in summer sun with mystic gleam in eyes.
Daddy Dear, Daddy Dear, is the world really round?
Daddy Dear, after all your hard steady work please,
Daddy Dear, Rest in Peace.
I pray you are safe and sound.
Daddy Dear, I will always be your girl.

(Dedicated to Di and Cee)

Great Demise

I remember the worst day of my life
like it was a right now experience.
Never forget it. Saturday morning, August 16, 2003,
phone call came, saying "please come right away."
I went, only to be told my brother had been shot and
killed along with his devoted wife being molested,
suffocated, and strangled to death.
Our family home was filled with hysteria.
I was calmed with a natural extract my baby sister
obtained from neighborhood health food store,
knowing I would be in desperate need of something
to help ease my heart, soothe my soul, deplete
this pain.
Only by God's grace, am I able to go on without my
darling brother's physical presence.
In my wildest dream, in my worst nightmare, I could
never imagine hatred coward would dare take my
brother's life.
He is my handsome king, he is love of my life.
Ever since our elementary days, we enjoyed each
other's company, I still feel closer than close, a need
to bring his spirit nearer.
I taught him to dance, he became my show-off partner.
Being a "suavely outstanding" poet, enhanced my
being "passionate love poet."

Oh, how we love to recite with articulate diction.
Memorizing poetry of our favorite poets, Longfellow,
his "Stevenson" I still recite to this day.
Oh, my handsome knight, my fashionable gent,
"Dapper Dan" "Dan the Man," perpetually clean as
a whistle.
Diamonds and gold, designer cologne.
Always looking and smelling awesomely good.
Boy from S.E. D.C. hood, my everything.
Vacationing together, we traveled to Hollywood,
rubbed shoulders with the best entertainers, celeb-
rities, Phyllis Hyman, Oscar Brown, Jr., Melvin
Franklin, Eddie Kendricks, Smokey Robinson,
Chuck Brown, Gil Scott-Heron, and Brian Jackson,
to name a few.
I cry through my smiles, I smile through my tears
with loving
thoughts of you.
Never thought I could make it without you, my
dear brother.
Your spirit strong reminds me of our dreams and
plans across lands, you remain "Dan the Man."
I will always cry for you, don't you know, I love and
miss you so.

**(Dedicated in Sweet Memory of my brother, my
dance partner, my first playmate, Daniel Levi
Beverly, Jr.)**

My Private Entertainer

Oh, my sweeter than sweet sister.
Closer than close to my heart, I long to be together
once again.
You are a beautiful flower, sweet as a rose, always
there to share
    and care no matter the hour.
My Private Entertainer, automatic wit, dancing on
top of desk, only
    to twirl, jump to floor, and do a split.
Oh, my Private Entertainer, you would sing
like Aretha.
I can still hear you sing "Call Me" the moment you
get there or
"Respect" R E S P E C T, especially hearing you sing
and dance to
    "Sock it to me, sock it to me, sock it to me."
Every time I hear "Let's just kiss and say goodbye,"
I think of you,
    last song you sang me.
You introduced me to "Raspberry Beret" and your
baby Prince
    singing "Do Me," last but not least, your Fat and
Nasty Boy Luther
    singing "Bad Boy" or "A House is not a Home."

A great soul food cook, making best fried chicken in the whole wide
world and we could never get enough of your curry chicken and
dumplings.
Creating tasty birthday cakes in shape of astrological signs.
Open house for family, friends, parlor games whether lose or win.
Master cosmetologist, keeping hair styles intact, wet set, cornrows and beads, press and curl, blow dry curl, whatever your need.
Kind, caring, doing your best forgetting rest.
You are missed by many; I love you plenty.
My Private Entertainer.

(A Tribute for my beloved sister Bernadette Marita Helen Beverly)

Uniquely So

As we walked to school, you in second grade, me, fourth grade.
Walking up and over grassy hills and unpaved graveled roads, you, small for your age, me, big for my age, holding hands, taking long way around, just for me.
Long, long time ago, I still remember coming home from school, you missed crowded bus, with your serious elementary mind, caught next bus coming. Made it home from S.E. to N.W.
We marveled at the way you would do things you would do.
Putting together model cars, boats, ships, and airplanes.
Using instructions, you applied each piece where they were designed to be, never hearing pieces rattling inside models.
Gifted with working with your hands, building model homes out of Lincoln Logs.
Creating pulleys and motorized elevators as we watched in awe.
Mesmerized by your vibrant paint-by-number sets, which soon moved you to paint rooms in our family home and painting our grandmother's home interior.

As a special treat, at record speed you would run to Sears, bringing back a quarter pound of chocolate break-up, solid milk chocolate was your fave.

Chocolate ice cream, chocolate milk, chocolate chips, anything chocolate.

Ready for high school, you choose a vocational school, studying, drafting, taking it very serious, was awarded a five year scholarship to Catholic University School of Architecture Engineering.

We were so proud of you.

Filled with excitement, you traveled to France as an exchange student studying at Fontainebleau.

Always experiencing something new.

Continuing to work with your hands and creating ideas you designed and made boxes out of exotic woods, zebra, paddock, maple, mahogany, elm to name a few.

Wooden boxes turned into furniture, gorgeous handmade furniture, wooden shelves, chest, tables, stained-glass and wood room dividers, beautiful floor lamps, and table lamps with stained-glass shades.

For more than twenty years, you entered craft shows, winning awards and many fans.

Yeah, you built your house and studio in upstate New York enjoying quiet stillness of nature, whether bird watching or working in your blooming gardens of flowers and herbs.

Our siblings call you "Boy Genius," I now join in the chorus, Uniquely So.

(A Tribute for my brother Anthony Beverly)

Poem for Dawud

I long to see my brother again.
I miss laying my head in his chest,
　His hearty hugs were comforting best.
Always and forever a peaceable man.
Lovingly looking after his family, from
Grandmother, parents, siblings, wives,
　　children, cousins, other relatives, and friends.
We miss you tremendously.
I cry a river, chills make me shiver.
I hear my brother say, "No woman, No cry."
I hear my brother say, "Strengthen your body,
　　mind, and soul."
Remember righteous deeds we did together,
　　do more of these.
Gain knowledge to share.
For elders and children always show a special care.
Very important my dear family, exercise and
eat to live.

(In Memory of my baby brother Dawud Ahmed Akil)

Mind of Her Own

This way, that way, which way today?
Busy as a bee, be careful you don't want a sting.
Stands strong in her convictions.
Big, bright, beautiful, brown eyes, accents
illumination
    of her gorgeous smile.
High quality, lover of designer watches, jew-
elry, handbags,
    fashions and accessories.
Brave, witty, smart, and a lover of the arts.
Poet, storyteller, comedian, literary genius, and critic.
Quite adventurous indeed, very good all she
decides to do,
    she will succeed.
Mommy called her "Turtle." Sensitive
    and slow, once she gets her feet on the
    ground, she will become more confident
    and comfortable.
Loves to praise the Lord and praises
    the good He does.
Since her elementary days, I can
    still hear her singing "keep in
    mind that Jesus Christ has died
    for us and has risen from the dead,
    He is our saving grace, He is Lord
    of all ages."

Alleluia, praise Him!
Returning student, reaching for
    higher education, graduating
    this year, achieving honors.
Looking forward to our next outing
    together.
Love you a bushel and a peck and
    a hug around the neck.

(Tribute for my lovely sister Linda Beverly-Brown)

Royal Blue Rhapsody

Abide with great respect and
   admiration.
Perpetually held in high esteem, waiting
With grace marbled vestibule,
Blinging chandeliers foyers.
Elegant boldness in vibrant, colorful
   strength.
Oh, so strong with an aura of lilies,
   lilac, and lavender, luscious, sweet
   scent.
Nourishing great souls, embracing
   human generosity.
Sweet, kind, gracefully phenomenal.
Supply with sheer attractive elegance.
Bright, brilliant attractiveness,
   turning heads, folks stop and
   stare to grasp, to obtain
   dimensions of your full potential
   Royal Blue Rhapsody.

(For My Darling Sister Karen)

Night Nurse

How blessed we are to have
    a nurse in our family.
Saving lives with CPR, giving
    all she can.
Perpetually ready to lend a
    helping hand.
Kind, caring, and generous, even
    toward strangers.
Loving all the babies, especially
    her grands.
So many ways like her Mama,
    goes to church every Sunday
    and Holy Days, walk in her house,
    in the kitchen there she stands.
Her homemade apple pie, yummy
    best across lands.
Queen of parlor games, has a
    monopoly on rolling doubles.
She's a stand up comic, y'all, make
    you crack your side.
An excellent driver, especially if
    you like viewing country sides.
Yes, she is a lover of nature, dogs,
    cats, birds, butterflies, and
    waterfalls.

Keeps everything neat, tidy, and
    immaculately clean.
No wonder she is a twenty year
    breast cancer survivor, still
    taking care of her family and
    many others.

(A Poem for my Dear sister Donna Carter)

Melody in My Heart

Sweetness of you, darling
    serenades my soul, you, only you
    know songs I long to hear.
Whispers in my ear, whether far away or
    somewhere near.
Like pages of sheet music, notes dance across
    each page. Thrilling passion in my
feet, terrific melodic beat, even our senior age.
Stare into each other's eyes, sweet darling.
Stars shine, sparkling reveals I love you so much.
Makes me feel you love me, too, such a smooth,
    tender touch.
Caring and kind, you are fine, my handsome gent,
    truly easy on these eyes, my eye candy, yummy,
    sweet.
Absence makes the heart grow fonder.
I miss you, my darling, when we are apart,
    with every step yonder.
Angels hum a melody, "Come to Me Soon."
A violin is playing, a harp is swaying a romantic
    tune.
I do not understand all I feel.
I just know songs in my heart are real.
I pray forevermore our love will continue to soar.
We care to be humanitarians.

We care to be faith-filled.
We care about innocence of little children.
We care to let our light shine.
Oh, my handsome darling, I sing a
    sweet song for you, from melody
    you place in my heart.

Lisa Lisa

I wanna thank you, Daddy
For introducing me to
    Paul Laurence Dunbar
    in my early elementary years.
Waking me and my siblings
    in a booming voice of "Lisa, Lisa, bless de Lawd."
All your grandchildren bare witness as well.
Always thought poem title was
    "Lisa Lisa," found later "in the
    morning" rang our wake up bell.
A favorite I called my very own
    when you came home from work
    or just wanna comfort me
    "Little Brown Baby" you recited
    for my waiting ears with glee.
Daddy Dear, did you ever hear "Sympathy?"
I found it's Dunbar's fans' most favorite poem of all.
Title "I know why the Caged Bird Sings,"
Dr. Angelou's first memoir derived from lines in
    this famous poem.
Following Dunbar's poems bring strong salute to
    perpetually rise and stand tall.

(For Daddy)

Dear Children

It is your time to love yourself.
Be ever so grateful for all you
    have.
Please, dear children, pray before
    bedtime and each day when you
    wake.
Always hold close to you, three
    virtues: faith, hope, and charity
    remembering charity is love and
    love is best of all.
Make sure you are kind, loving, and
    brave.
Forever, know you are loved.
I love you. Auntie Di Di

(A Tribute to Words on Wednesday
dedicated to Khadi)

The Year 2563

I am an ancestor over five
   hundred years.
My distinctive studio is a
   shadowed space station.
I no longer wear bright ruby
   red lipstick.
Occasionally, a little lip gloss
   or Vaseline will do.
My total assets are at a bare
   minimum.
It is better to give than receive.
Seems horses and dogs are
   extinct.
Nothing much left but scattered
   skeletons and fossils.
Over twenty-seven ancestors
   quietly sit in my company.
I am only one being interviewed.
I talk endlessly, I have so much
   to say.
Actually, I do not have a care in
   the world.

Sweet Jaded Jewel

Sweet Jaded Jewel
My heart goes out to you.
I feel for you, Sweet Jade.
Many mighty miseries you
    have felt
Multifarious discomforts you
    have endured.
I wonder, Sweet Jade, what do
    you feel?
What marvelous main tool brought
    you through?
I am so happy you are able to
    slowly get out and about.
Wear mask, gloves, wash your
    hands frequently, no crowds.
Living alone myself, I know empty
    feeling of loneliness.
Especially when you are unable
    to get up and out.
Sweet Jaded Jewel, hearing your
    story, I vision myself on my own
    living alone.
My tool, my saving grace is power
    of prayer and poetry.

(For One Who Survived COVID)

Fabulous Friends

Fantastic, fabulous feelings
  flow from Fabulous Friends!
True fond friendship, dear to our hearts
Together for decades, never acknowledging
  being apart.
Creating precious, endearing
  memories happy, awesome start.
Fabulous Friends!
A bond of mutual affection, admiration, dedication
  wonderful sensations, sincere, darling, dear
devotions.
Warm, fuzzy feelings, even over phone.
Fabulous Friends!
Oh, beautiful friend of mine, you for me, me for you,
  makes me oh so happy.
My love for you, heavenly as stars above
True understanding loads of love,
  a comfort friends feel like an exotic island's cove.
Reminiscing on years gone by
  kindness, inspiration, laughter
  blessed memories reasons why.
Through ups, downs, safe sound
  together forever we are found.
Fabulous Friends!
Ecstatic to see each other, grand time to share
A friend like my forever friend is to have someone who
  perpetually cares.

(Dedicated to Angela Wilson Turnbull)

With A Child's Heart

I see you with a child's heart
So darling, delightful
Mighty, mighty insightful
Heavenly humanitarian.
Sweet, glorious blessing, I
    gratefully call you my dear
    dear friend.
Spirit runs freely, as adventurously
    you traveled east to west,
Drive away cars premiered test.
Brave warrior girl, giving your
    ecstatic best.
Attracted to warmth, water, and
    wineries
Connected to rolling Russian
    rivers and ravishing Redwoods'
    luscious hues of burgundy.
Loving nature's sunrise to sunsets
Camp fire scenes, fulfilling dreams
    feeling lighthearted and carefree,
    singing with a child's heart.

(Dedicated to Liz Larew)

Friendship Like Ours

In my mind's eye, colorful bouquets of
    forget-me-nots beautifully unite our
    sensitive souls.
Standing in a massive field of beautiful,
    bright bountiful sunflowers.
Oh, how thrilling, our friendship strengthens
    as years rush by hours after hours.
Fond, strong memories of entertaining ourselves
    and many others, including internationally.
Especially times of contentment and ardent, silly
laughter.
Perpetually, we support eachother's endeavors,
each other's
    dreams.
Knowing God is in the midst of our sunshine and
all we do.
Friends forever, finding our hearts reuniting over
and over again.
Pondering, collaborating helps to reach long and
short term goals.
A sassy friendship to have and behold.
Times together like mother and daughter sitting at
elders' feet.
Other times, like big sister like little sister helping
to overcome
    defeats.

Smiling over phone, no matter distances.
Serious as we are, we forever appreciate each other's words
   of existence.
Grateful for a perpetual, loving friendship like ours.

(Dedicated to Angela Wilson Turnbull)

Crying Heart

Haiku #619

Oh my cardboard heart
Sounds extremely treacherous
Love Pillow Comforts.

Rid COVID

Haiku #1230

Please cleanse atmosphere
We will not have to wear masks
We can hug again.

Poems and Lovers

How does it make you feel is the question?
Love in form of Valentine hearts. Poetic passion
    pleases perpetually.
Seeps deep into hearts of lovers.
Ardently gives comforting feelings of love,
    so wondrously.
Pleasantly unite hearts with everlasting glee,
    oh, sweet poetry.
Endearing poetry love, far beyond our eyes can see.
Memories, shared smiles of grace beyond fascinating years.
Forever remembering grand goodness.
Melodic songs, melodies pure and true.
Every waking moment, there's a sweet poem waiting
to be shared.
Love poems, dear to lovers' hearts.
Expressing sweet goodness of love, just for the asking.
Love shaped in form of poetry.
Love touches lover's hearts, energizes lover's
sole being.
Lovers feel live and strong beyond infinite years.
Positive, poetic passions, lovers feel love of poetry.

It's Your Anniversary

Sweet, unconditional love enhancing each other's
desires strong,
    sweet, satisfying.

Looking back like Sankofa, planting seeds, stepping
steadily, gayly
    towards a continuous royal life together.

Feels good, surge of warmth, feel tantalizing fire,
fragrant desire of
    candles aflame, two hearts, holding hands,
looking into each
    other's eyes.

Stare infinitely, deeply into future, continuously
making memories,
    feeling essence of days gone by.

Happy to see you are still here with love of your life,
best friends
    humming love songs, praying to perpetually
stay in love.

Loving the feeling only true love, mutual love, ever-
lasting love can
    bring, always and forever.

Watching the sun set, wishing upon twinkling stars,
thankful for
 twilit skies, while dancing and twirling beneath
thrill of full moon.

It's your anniversary!

(Dedicated to Diane and Eric)

Fossil of Love

You wrote your destination on my heart!
Only thing that gets me up is being by your side
You being with me is what I like
Tasty treat, yummy treat you are
Hunter gets captured by the game
I've known many not many captured
have known me
Round Brown tantalizing
You will never lose your power
Fantastic, sensational thrill
You will always have something
Phenomenal
Your love is tear jerking
Tears come at will
Tears of satisfaction, tears of joy
Release me, unchain my heart

My First Love

We loved each other so much.
We knew, felt each other's love.
My first love...only one first is given
to thee.
Like dandelions wisp in warm
Summer breeze...gone.
Oh, how I longed for the gentleness
of your touch once again.
I will forever remember your smile.
Your laughter deeply tickled
my soul...bold to have and behold.
Promises aching, broken like my
heart by my first love.

Desirous Passions

If ever you should wonder
    my darling dear sweetheart,
    know I love you so.
I love you with a vibrancy of keenest
    rainbow you will ever know.
I love hand dancing with you, how you
    twirl me and twirl me pull me into you,
    oh honey, never, ever let me go.
Feels satisfying when you do loving things
    you do.
Forever true I am amazingly grateful for
    sweet love you perpetually give, I hope you
    feel how strong my love is for you.
My heart is warm, my love is strong, whether
    near or far, I love being where you are.
You set my soul on fire, my heart's desire.
I will always safeguard my heart and soul with
    desirous passions just for you.

Looking for Mister Ten

Tall, dark, and handsome sounds
  about right.
Righteous, caring goodness,
  a strong-willed might.
A good, loving spirit and gentleman
  at heart.
Tantalizing kisses at quiet nights'
  end or vibrant days' start.
A look of love, desirous, loving it
  intent in his eyes.
My darling dandy, sweet as candy
Got to be an athlete and scholar
Perpetual brilliance makes me
  wanna holler
A man as gorgeous is sure to win
Oh my, I have found my "Mister Ten."

TLC LEMON POUND CAKE

TLC lemon butter pound
Whipped by hand in stainless steel
bowl and wooden spoon.
Whip it, fluff it, listen to music.
New kitchen aid sitting to
side,
Old fashioned way feels good to my stride.
Blending little at a time
For very dear friend of mine
Makes me oh so happy.
It's been many years.
Aroma oozed all over this camp.
When cake comes out of oven, it is sure
to be a champ.
I had to whip up this cake as buttery
as it can be.
A sweet, moist lemon pound cake.
Made with tender loving care, you see.
A cake for a king, champion, celebrity.
Returns, homeward bound
Never forgetting his plateau's grounds.

(For Kwame)

Misty Eyes

Strong sentiments of serious care
comforts my mind, heart and soul.
Eases my spirit, brings feelings of
sincere love.
Agape love, love with sensational
care, good feelings knowing you
are there, knowing you truly care.
Strengthens my sole being.
I can walk better, I can see clearer,
I can carry on.
Silent tears roll down my face.
Tears of joy and happiness.
You make my eyes Misty.

ABOUT THE AUTHOR

Sylvia Dianne Beverly
"Ladi Di"

Sylvia Dianne Beverly is a native of Southeast Washington, D.C. and alumni of Anacostia H.S. and The University of District of Columbia. She is an internationally acclaimed poet, presenting poetry in Brixton, London, England, at the Lewisham Theater. A collection of her work is housed at George Washington University's Gelman Library. She is a member of A Splendid Wake, Gelman Library, George Washington University.

Also, she has been featured at the Smithsonian's Museum of History, African Arts Museum, Hirshhon Museum and other Smithsonians. Ladi Di, as she is affectionally called, is a founding member of the poetry ensemble "Collective Voices " and has presented at many schools, libraries, churches, radio stations, and television stations. One of her most memorable presentations is at a private tea with Former Ambassador of South Africa for the United States, Franklin A. Sonn. Along with her poetry ensemble, she has presented at the Italian Embassy and the Arts Museum in N.W., Washington, D.C. for Maryland State Poet Laureate Grace Cavalieri. Ladi

Di celebrated the fortieth anniversary of Host Grace Cavalieri, reading on her show, "The Poet and the Poem," at the Library of Congress Experience.

Also, she is a founding member of the Anointed PENS (Poets Empowered to Nurture Souls) Poetry Ministry, out of Ebenezer AME Church, an alumnus of Poets in Progress with Poet Laureate of District of Columbia, the late Dolores Kendrick. She was a facilitator of Poetry Club at Harmony Hall Regional Center for fifteen years until COVID-19. Ladi Di is the founder/director of Girls and Boys with Hearts youth poetry group. She is the author of two books, *Forever In Your Eyes* and *Cooking Up South*. Both books may be found on Amazon. Her poetry is in many anthologies, with the most recent being the *25th Annual Poetry Ink Anthology*, Moonstone Press, and *Protest 2021, 100 Thousand Poets for Change*.

Ladi Di is also called "Love Poet." She loves to teach and share. The late Dr. Maya Angelou is her hero. She is the proud matriarch of her family. Celebrating Black history 2018, she and her family received, posthumously for her dad, a Congressional gold medal from the United States Marines. Her most recent honor is Prince George's County Poet of Excellence, 2020. Even more recent, her poetry is presented in "Sailor's Review," October 2021, out of Zimbabwe, South Africa, and an interview in "Sailor's Review," November 2021. Due to her long time dedication for the literary arts, she has been named "Literary Leader" for Prince George's County, Maryland. Ladi Di is available for in person and

Sylvia Dianne Beverly

virtual presentation at your next celebration. Poetry is her passion.

syladydi@comcast.net.

Sylvia Beverly on Facebook

WHAT PEOPLE ARE SAYING ABOUT SYLVIA AND "A Kiss of Curiosity"

Just when we need it the most, Ladi Di, the Love Poet, delivers verse of reflection, remembrance, and challenge. In "A Kiss of Curiosity," she presents herself, and all of us, as life-long learners. Her sound, her specifics, and, yes, her abundant love for others, this life, and her God will stay with readers long after they turn the last page of these delicious "knick knacks" of language and heart. Treat your heart to these poems. You'll be grateful you did.
- Sally Toner, author of Anansi and Friends from Finishing Line Press

Sylvia Dianne "Ladi Di" Beverly is a rare soul. A poet's poet. Her work is heartfelt. Stunning. Necessary. An incredible wordsmith, she is blessed with the remarkable gift of discernment. Whether extolling the virtues of gratitude for the little things or exploring broader life issues, her poems overflow with hope and possibility. A poet par excellence, she infuses her writing with deep spirituality and expresses her convictions with vulnerability and authenticity. "Ladi Di" writes poetry that is a healing balm for the mind, body, and spirit. You will

feel inspired after reading her latest book, "A Kiss of Curiosity."
- **Dr. Michael Anthony Ingram is the host and producer of the Quintessential Listening: Poetry Online Radio podcast.**

To read Sylvia Beverly's poetry is to experience the strength of love of humanity and heritage that this writer brings to her work. Whether she is writing about a first trip to New York, a memory of her father, or a meditation on slavery, Beverly blends thought and action into each poem, inviting the reader to reflect and respond to her words.
- **Joanna Howard**

Genuine. The poems in "A Kiss of Curiosity" are the real thing. Yes, their dance, their concern and their love will all come up on your porch to sit with you for a while. Enjoy their visit.
— **Hiram Larew, Mud Ajar (Atmosphere Press, 2021)**

She's more than Ladi Di; she's my loving aunt.
I gave her a symbol and it's "The Phoenix Rising" as nothing can hold her down or back. I tell her she's been my inspiration since I've known the definition of inspire. Her poetry is sure to uplift. Our family has a treasure and we know it. We love her way with words and her passion for love itself. She moves mountains and gives hope to those souls she crosses on a daily. Just like Maya Angelou, her

favorite, she is phenomenal. Ladi Di's poetry brings charm, quality, and dedication to this craft.
Niece
Dayo A. Beverly
PARTNER **Blueshore**

"With so much turmoil and trouble in our world, it's comforting to read and hear the poems of Ladi Di. Love streams through her passages whether it's "When I think of my Father" or "Moon Lit Love." It is often said that "love is the answer". Well, you understand how true that is as you read Ladi Di's poetry. In line after line and poem after poem, her loving words abide. I applaud her writing and her loving heart.»
Curtis Crutchfield
News Anchor
CTV

TRIBUTE POEMS FOR
THE AUTHOR

MY SOUL SISTER SWINGS HIGH–FOR LADI DI

Queen of Spoken Word–Ladi Di
hails from the nation's capital
welding divine voice, illuminating vision, well fought
victory for our people–Black Goddess Warrior Woman.

Statuesque, brilliant, beautiful a livening you like
so many of our African Queen Mothers pour into
our souls, one with the Holy Spirit.

Your love lyrics, prose invoke "clutch your heart"
cultural memory causes us to regain lost ances-
tral strength.

You Ladi Di
quenches our thirst with your vibrant veracity–a
resident truth sayer a sister girl who gives us all she
is and has. a woman whose integrity spans the globe
your name is spoken by the masses you are
known in our homes, and our hearts, families, and
communities.

You grace audiences from DC, VA, MD, (the world)
poetry readings, workshops to
radio, T.V, to fully choreographed, 60's Black Arts
Movement poet's resurrection electrifying thou-
sands at Brixton Academy, WE REAL COOL back in
the day–remember us blowing up the stage, blowing
up the stage over and over beginning in the late
90's–a standing ovation like no other!
U.S. BLACK FEMALE POETS "CV" TAKE U.K.
AUDIENCES BY STORM–BAM!!!

My defender, my protector, my most precious God-
center big sister.
Your mom always knew we were close as Coretta Scott
King and Betty Shabazz you inspire me each day
taking the good over all things lifting us up even
when you yourself could use a kind comfort a word,
a prayer, praise–a hand to hold you gave us even
more...teaching the children, our babies, memori-
alizing our people, nourishing our bodies with your
tantalizing good home "up south" cooking.

We performed from embassies, to House of Ruth,
Carter Barron, literary conferences, Smithsonian's
American History Museum with Sonia and Sweet
Honey, universities like UDC with J. California
Cooper, to schools with hundreds of children, wed-
dings, art galleries, rooftop parties, political ral-
lies, It's Your Mug, Mr. Henry's, Takoma Station,
Capital Book Festivals, to libraries for the DC Arts
Commission, to nursing homes for our elders, to the

Hyltons for our London funding party to your literary collections capturing DC Poet's finest at GW– you stand out among us all.

Remember those late night rehearsals at Sankofa, their opening to prep for our revolutionary protest performance in London–the all night after party– guys chasing after you like their breath needed refilling! It's true y'all know what I'm talking about!

Your precious performances held us close, your anthologies mended our truths as one, your book publications and launch events blew out record sales drawing huge audiences and most notably your faithful survival my sister–your triumphant treatments–your taking it all–your strength–girt– grace–sometimes silent walks with God
wrapped you up in His loving arms
brought you to ring that bell my sister and carry you home back to us again and again and again.

For the love you give, the stories you bind in our hearts, our modern day Maya -the sister girl friend who lends you her laughter when you can't smile. Who plays your life back to you when you can no longer remember.

Who shows up to care for your only girl child to give her the "most funniest" day of her four-year-old life. When Christiana was only four you took her among the ocean creatures, slides and bus rides

from upper northwest DC to Baltimore and back.
That's you Ladi Di, you dropped everything for my
baby when no one else would.

Ladi Di, you are the one who stands between God
and the devil, brings us on the right side of things
away from people who act a fool and can't do no
better, you know who I am talking about!

This sister is undeniable.
This sister is incomparable.
This sister right here is unprecedented.

Her faith penetrates our hearts brings you back
from death.
If you are lucky enough to be loved by her you know
what a taste of heaven is really like each time, each
time, each time you are with her–miracles enfold you.
That's you Ladi Di!

That's my sister girl–Ladi Di
My bestie poet, mama, auntie, big sis, sacred soul
Sylvia Dianne Beverly,
God's glamour girl extraordinaire!

Who stands with me in these knowings of you?

Who–stands–with–me–in–these -knowings–of–you?

All of us and especially this family, these friends,
Brother Ah, Kwame, me, your Mommy, Daddy,

sisters, brothers, nieces, nephews, Khadi, BRENARDO , CV, DC's 80's, 90's, 2000's poetry, and creative arts community and all those with us in London, England.

You rock the world–Ladi Di

You live in my heart forever!

(© **Angela Wilson Turnbull–June 30, 2021–Read to Ladi Di Live at Carlyle's July 6, 2021-Performed March 14, 2022 at Ladi Di's 73rd Birthday Celebration at Public House, National Harbor MD (References: UDC, University of the District of Columbia GW, George Washington University, and CV Collective Voices, Original Washington, DC Based Women's Poetry Collective)**

Today

Today I walked past my mirror.
I caught a glimpse of my family in my face
Some of those who are still on this side of glory
And some who have gone on to be in an unfathomably better place
It took me aback, so I shouted out loud, "Thank you, Most High God for the lovely memories of those I love and for giving me another wondrous day in the race!"
Pretty brown Ladi Di, Queen
It was your eyes that showed up in my reflection and manifested this freestyle to you.
I pray it resonates with you like the sweetest, moist, most delicious cupcake you could ever taste.
Deep, round pools of love, light, and passion
My inspiration, my whimsical creative joy
Thank you for being a safe space behind my lids.
I can see you posing with a hand on your hip.
Reading poetry, draped beautiful fashions.
Enunciating rhythmic words with such style and grace
I miss you dearly Ladi Di, today, tomorrow, forever more
I'm sending you peace and good vibrations filled with telepathic warm hugs just for you to embrace.
I thought I'd try and lift myself up and bless you with a freestyle.

(©Nichole Holland)

Love Poem For a Ladi

A birthday tribute for Sylvia Dianne "Ladi Di" Beverly
(originally written 3/15/2014, revised and presented to Ladi Di on Friday, March 11, 2022) © J. Joy "Sistah Joy" Matthews Alford

Cruising through life in first gear
Wanna hear all the sounds
See all the sights Smell all the roses
Keepin' my toes toasty
In my fiery red boots
So I can hit the road
On a moment's notice
Cause that's the way I roll
Smiles perpetually are my attire
Free-flowing tears affirm the fire
Confirms that Jesus dwells inside
Keepin' my heart yearning
For His light and love So I lift His Word
Ensuring it's heard wherever I go
Leaving a trail of loving-kindness
Light and billowy
Like sunflowers in sunshine
For friend or foe to follow
While discovering the joys of life
So, my sister, on this day hope you don't mind
That I stepped inside your mind
Pulled forth a few lines

A Kiss of Curiosity

Let them fly upon this Potomac breeze
Just to set them free
Share a moment or two
From one sister to another
From one who knows
How good words of love feel
When shared from warm and gentle places
Sweet and kind places of the heart.